The Library of
ASTRONAUT BIOGRAPHIES™

ALAN SHEPARD

The First American in Space

Tamra B. Orr

rosen
central™

The Rosen Publishing Group, Inc., New York

Published in 2004 by The Rosen Publishing Group, Inc.
29 East 21st Street, New York, NY 10010

First Edition

Library of Congress Cataloging-in-Publication Data

Orr, Tamra.
Alan Shepard: The First American in Space / Tamra B. Orr. — 1st ed.
    v. cm. — (The library of astronaut biographies)
Includes bibliographical references and index.
Contents: A decade of contrasts—The launching of a future
astronaut—The Mercury 7 astronauts—Freedom 7—The terror
and triumph of Apollo—Into the business world—A quiet ending.
ISBN 0-8239-4455-7 (library binding)
1. Shepard, Alan B. (Alan Bartlett), 1923–1998—Juvenile literature.
2. Astronauts—United States—Biography—Juvenile literature.
[1. Shepard, Alan B. (Alan Bartlett), 1923–1998 2. Astronauts.] I.
Title. II. Series.
TL789.85.S5O77 2004
629.45'0092—dc21

                                                      2003010703

Manufactured in the United States of America

CONTENTS

A DECADE OF CONTRASTS

America in the 1920s was a study in contrasts. Brilliant and modern inventions were being created even as the country remained rooted in an agrarian and rural tradition. Young men and women—"swells" and "flappers"—danced to the wild new sounds of jazz and became drunk on illegal alcohol, scandalizing their parents' generation, which tried to reimpose some old-fashioned morality. The postwar economy was booming, but the greatest stock market crash in history soon followed. The period called the Roaring

Pioneering aviator Charles Lindbergh flies into Croydon Airport, completing the first-ever solo flight across the Atlantic Ocean on May 29, 1927. Alan Shepard was only four years old at the time of this flight, but Lindbergh became one of his lifelong heroes and inspired him to take to the skies.

Twenties was a fascinating time, and in 1923 Alan B. Shepard Jr. became a part of it. He entered the world on November 18 of that year, the son of Alan Bartlett Shepard Sr., a retired army colonel and businessman, and Renza Emerson Shepard. Alan Jr. would grow up on the family farm in East Derry, New Hampshire, an eighth-generation New Englander.

As the 1920s began, World War I had just ended. The United States had been spared the kind of devastation experienced by the warring European nations, which had fought longer and lost more men and would recover far more slowly. The U.S. economy rebounded quickly. Soon leisure time—and the money to spend on it—was plentiful. Thanks to Henry Ford and his new concept of mass production, automobiles were now available for about $290 and were quickly gaining in popularity. The concept of credit—purchasing goods with the promise to pay for them later—was flourishing. Why pay now when you could pay later? In the peacetime economy, people suddenly had more time and money, and more ways to spend both.

Though the time, money, and consumer goods suddenly in abundance for some Americans created a new sense of freedom and energy, a more puritanical trend was also developing. Social reformers had long been arguing that alcohol was an evil that resulted in many social problems, including poverty, domestic violence, crime, and poor health. As a result, they felt it should be outlawed, and their campaign was successful. The new decade saw the passing of the Volstead Act and eventually the Eighteenth Amendment, which made it illegal to sell, manufacture, or transport any kind of nonmedicinal alcohol—including beer and wine—anywhere in the United States.

This period, which came to be called Prohibition, accomplished some of the goals it intended and far more that it did not. While alcohol consumption went down, crime actually went up as illegal trade on alcohol developed. Saloons closed and speakeasies opened—places where only the right password got a person through the door and alcohol was frequently served in coffee cups. Organized crime and powerful gangsters like Al Capone were another direct result of Prohibition—a side effect no one could have predicted. Much like the drug trade of today, the struggle to gain control of the illegal alcohol market

World-famous magician and escape artist Harry Houdini hangs from a hook and frees himself from a straitjacket on March 30, 1916. Known as the "Genius of Escape Who Will Startle and Amaze," Houdini also dabbled in aviation. In 1910, he was proclaimed the first person to sustain flight over Australia.

created criminals who dominated and controlled entire communities. They did so with guns in their hands and greed in their hearts.

In the 1920s, women were often referred to as "dames" and "dolls" at the very same time that they first obtained the vote and entered the workplace in a variety of jobs. In a time when stiff and formal ballroom dancing was still the norm in polite society, sweaty and exhausting dance marathons that lasted for hours and hours were the new craze among young men and women who performed the frenzied moves of the Charleston and the shimmy. The passion for loud music and frantic dancing resulted in the decade often being referred to as the Roaring Twenties or the Jazz Age. Other popular entertainment included watching baseball games, tuning in to the radio for the Miss America contest, or reading about the amazing feats of renowned magician and escape artist Harry Houdini.

Presidents of the decade included Woodrow Wilson (1913–1921), Warren G. Harding (1921–1923), Calvin Coolidge (1923–1929), and Herbert Hoover (1929–1933). Harding focused on business and restoring the country to the relatively stable and prosperous condition it was in before the beginning of World War I. A great deal of legislation was passed during the early 1920s that helped to encourage the growth and success of American businesses in the hope of jump-starting the postwar economy. Harding's decisions were quite popular with a country in need of both growth and stability, so it was an emotional blow when he died unexpectedly of a blood clot in San Francisco in 1923. Following his death, it was revealed that Harding's administration was corrupt, engaging in bribes and misuse of public funds. Vice President Calvin Coolidge finished out Harding's term and was easily reelected to the presidency the following year.

The 1920s did not only roar with the energy of carefree youth. It also roared with the darker forces of social strife and change. The Ku Klux Klan, a violent and racist organization dedicated to making the United States a whites-only Christian nation, grew in size and power during this decade. Some of the most important civil rights activists of the future were born in the 1920s, including Martin Luther King Jr. and Malcolm X.

In 1925, the growing debate between evolution and creation science (a literal interpretation of the biblical Creation story) escalated, as a southern biology teacher named John Scopes was put on trial for daring to teach the theory of evolution in his classroom. The issues raised by the Scopes Monkey Trial were fiercely debated for decades and continue even today in some school districts.

American physicist Dr. Robert H. Goddard stands next to the first liquid-propelled rocket just before its launch on March 16, 1926, in Auburn, Massachusetts. In a 1920 report to the Smithsonian Institution, Goddard first proposed the possibility of a rocket flight to the Moon. He was widely mocked for what seemed like an outlandish idea.

Following World War I, a nation already divided by racial conflict, social change, and sharp ideological debate was further strained by a large increase in immigration. A record number of immigrants began to pour into the United States until the National Origins Act of 1924 was passed, putting a cap on how many foreigners could enter the country. Americans feared that if immigration was not restricted, too many jobs would go to foreigners who were willing to work for less money than most Americans. This in turn might drive down wages for millions of American workers. In reaction to this fear, the number of immigrants allowed to enter the country was limited to 164,000 per year. This limit was further reduced to 150,000 three years later.

As the decade wore on, the strong postwar economy began to run out of steam. Industrial and agricultural production began to fall steadily, while unemployment continued to rise. As the Roaring Twenties came to a close, the biggest financial catastrophe in history struck. It was October 29, 1929—the day that would later be referred to as Black Tuesday. The great stock market crash shocked the country. Overnight, wealthy people became poor, and panic spread throughout the cities. It was the beginning of the Great Depression, a decade-long economic downturn during which poverty became an everyday fact of life for many people. An increasing number of workers lost their jobs, and bread and soup kitchens were established to help those who were not

This is the cover of a 1929 issue of the science fiction magazine *Amazing Stories*. The image depicts a scene from H. G. Wells's story *War of the Worlds*, in which aliens attack Earth.

able to survive without basic assistance. Banks all across the nation closed. To help soften some of the blow of this widespread suffering and to jolt the economy, Prohibition and the Eighteenth Amendment were repealed. It was again legal to buy, sell, and drink alcohol. The Depression would linger into the 1940s until another world war would once again spur the U.S. economy into action.

Hard times called for inexpensive entertainment and escapism. Perhaps that is why science fiction stories and books began to have such a strong impact on society in the 1930s. Stories of rocket travel to the Moon and planets began appearing in new science fiction magazines, such as *Amazing Stories* and *Weird Tales*, which were eagerly bought by readers of all ages. Edgar Rice Burroughs, best known for his Tarzan series, was publishing such classics as *At the Earth's Core* (1922) and *The Moon Men* (1926), while Ray Cummings was writing *Brigands of the Moon* (1931). Buck Rogers and Flash Gordon were outer-space heroes who caught the fancy of many young people whose imaginations had already been fueled by aviator Charles Lindbergh's historical solo flight across the Atlantic Ocean in 1927.

One of those children who was deeply inspired by the possibilities of flight was Alan Shepard Jr. Little did he know as he went about his chores on his family's farm that one day his name would appear in newspapers all over the world, just like Lindbergh's. Instead of being the first man to fly over the ocean, however, Shepard would be the first American to fly into outer space.

CHAPTER 1

THE LAUNCHING OF A FUTURE ASTRONAUT

Alan Shepard had a storybook childhood in many ways. Born on November 18, 1923, he was raised on his family's New Hampshire farm, doing chores and going to school in one of the country's last one-room schoolhouses. Six grades all met in a single room, with a total of less than thirty students. In later years, when Shepard was interviewed about his early education, he recalled it with great affection and appreciation: "[W]hen I was in the one-room county school, my ambition was just to get through with a creditable performance." Shepard seemed to exceed his modest goals by completing kindergarten through sixth

Alan Shepard enjoyed an idyllic American childhood, complete with farm chores, a paper route, a one-room schoolhouse, and a job at a local airfield that introduced him to flight.

grade in only five years. "I'd like to say I was smart enough to finish six grades in five years," said Shepard in an interview with Achievement.org, "but I think perhaps the teacher was just glad to get rid of me."

It's not surprising that Alan's favorite subjects in school were math and science. He had one teacher who particularly inspired him at the same time that she intimidated him. "She was about nine feet tall, as I recall," he told the Achievement.org interviewer, "and a very tough disciplinarian. That's the lady that taught me how to study and really provided that kind of discipline, which is essentially still with me."

Along with school and chores at home, Alan had a regular paper route. He used the money he earned from it to buy a bicycle. In his adult years, he often reflected on these early days and felt that the combination of school, work, and family all helped him become an astronaut. He told Achievement.org, "I think the sense of family and family achievement, plus the discipline which I received there from that one-room school were really helpful in what I did later on."

Dreams of Flight

Once he had earned enough money to buy his bike, Alan rode it 10 miles (16 kilometers) every Saturday morning to the local airport. There he cleaned out hangars and helped to push airplanes in and out of them. He spent many hours at the airport soaking up everything related to aviation that he could. This sparked his lifelong interest in airplanes and a passion for flight. Lindbergh's transatlantic flight in May 1927 made the idea of flying even more alluring. The pilot had flown 3,610 miles (5,810 km) from New York to Paris in just under thirty-four hours, nonstop.

"I think that my interest in aviation goes back to grade school, nine, ten, early teens," Shepard told Achievement.org. "When Lindbergh made his flight, he was the big hero. I started building model airplanes."

The very first plane ride young Alan ever took was in a homemade glider that he and his friend made. They only got 4 feet (1.2 m) off the ground before crashing. His next trip into the air occurred while he was working at the airport. After a great deal of begging and pleading, one of the pilots took him on several flights. Shepard was even given the chance to handle the plane's controls. A future astronaut was born.

In the 1930s, there were not any official aviation schools, and money for additional education was scarce. The effects of the Depression were still in full force, and less than 10 percent of high school graduates ever went on to college. However, Alan's father had a plan. Alan Shepard Sr. spoke with a friend who was a U.S. Naval Academy graduate. He told him about his son's passion for science and aviation. The friend suggested that young Alan study and then take the entrance exams to the U.S. Naval

Academy. If he passed, he could become a naval officer and then go to flight school. "I guess I did apply myself properly," said She-pard. "I passed the entrance exams, got the appointment, and that's how it all started."

A portrait of Alan Shepard as a cadet at the Admiral Farragut Academy in 1941. Farragut is a college preparatory school whose graduates often go on to the United States Naval Academy.

Alan graduated from the Pinkerton Academy in Derry, in 1940. He then spent a year at the Admiral Farragut Academy in Toms River, New Jersey. The next step was the U.S. Naval Academy, where he took the very first footsteps that would one day lead to the stars.

In the Navy

The next ten years of Shepard's life were busy, exciting, and challenging ones. As he had hoped, he

Alan Shepard is shown here as a member of the U.S. Naval Academy crew team. Shepard graduated from the academy in 1944 as World War II was winding down.

entered the United States Naval Academy at Annapolis, Maryland, and threw himself into both his studies and sports. He became a member of the varsity crew team and is remembered by most classmates as a very likable person. He graduated 462nd out of a class of 913 in June 1944. Although World War II was winding down, he was still sent to be an ensign aboard the destroyer USS *Cogswell*, deployed in the Pacific Ocean.

A few months later, the war ended. Before Shepard started on the next step in his education, he took a moment to marry Louise Brewer from Pennsylvania, whom he had met while at the U.S. Naval Academy. The two were married on March 3, 1945, and stayed together for the rest of their lives, raising three daughters.

Top Gun

Shepard began training as an aviator in 1945. He was taught at a naval air station in Corpus Christi, Texas, as well as one in Pensacola, Florida. He was so eager

At the end of World War II, Alan Shepard married Louise Brewer of Kennett Square, Pennsylvania. The ceremony took place on March 3, 1945.

to get his official naval wings that he took additional lessons at a local civilian flying school along with his regular classes. As a result, he soon earned his wings in March 1947.

Now that he could fly, Shepard's life began to surge forward in many ways. He served with the 42nd Fighter Squadron on an aircraft carrier in Norfolk, Virginia, and Jacksonville, Florida. He served several tours of duty in the Mediterranean and was soon considered one of the navy's top test pilots. His job was to fly experimental planes and perform high-altitude test flights. During Shepard's time with the 42nd Squadron, he flew everything from the F4D Skyray, F3H Demon, and F8U Crusader to the F11F Tigercat, F2H3 Banshee, and F5D Skylancer. His duties ranged from testing in-flight fueling systems (the transfer of fuel from one airborne plane to another during high-speed flights) to gathering data on the light at different altitudes and reporting on the variety of air masses over the North American continent. Shepard was also one of the first pilots ever to test landing procedures on the navy's new angled-deck aircraft carriers.

"Shepard was as curious in the air as he was on the ground," wrote John Moore, a fellow test pilot and friend of Shepard's, in the July 28, 1998, issue of *Florida Today*. "He took off one day in an F4D Skyray (a beautiful fighter plane) with full external fuel tanks and wanted to determine its roll rate in that configuration. And he found out the roll rate was much faster at the completion of the roll because both external tanks had enough of that foolishness and flew off the Skyray landing in a farmer's field with no harm to anyone but Douglass Aircraft [the maker of the Skyray]," he continued. "The fittings were redesigned. Just another day in the life of Al Shepard, test pilot and boy wonder . . . Al was an exceptional man, a natural hero, yet seemingly unaffected by fame."

In Tom Wolfe's classic historical novel about the space program, *The Right Stuff* (1979), he described Shepard as a "top-notch Navy aviator, tough, quick-witted and a leader." Many colleagues and instructors also noted Shepard's dedication to his work. After only one tour of squadron duty and at a far younger age than most officers, he was chosen as a candidate for test pilot school.

Above and Beyond

In 1950, Shepard entered the United States Navy Test Pilot School in Patuxent River, Maryland. From 1953 to 1956, he was assigned as the operations officer of 193rd Fighter Squadron based in Moffett Field, California. His squadron was a night fighter unit that flew Banshee jets.

Two F2H3 Banshee jets of the kind Lieutenant Commander Alan Shepard (shown in navy uniform, inset) flew in test pilot school in Maryland and during fighter squadron duty in California and the western Pacific. These jets are flying over Wonsan Harbor in North Korea in 1953, looking for enemy targets to attack during the Korean War.

During this period, he logged more than 8,000 hours of flying time, including 3,700 hours in jet aircraft. With the 193rd Squadron, Shepard did two tours of duty in the western Pacific on the aircraft carrier USS *Oriskany*. Afterward, he returned to the U.S. Navy Test Pilot School and worked as an instructor.

Not many navy pilots were as driven as Shepard. He said, "Obviously, I was challenged by becoming a naval aviator, by landing aboard aircraft carriers and so on. But in those days, I figured I was just one of those guys that was doing his job. Maybe I could roll the airplane a little better than the next guy. But when I was selected, after my very first tour of squadron duty, to become one of the youngest candidates for the test pilot school, I began to realize, 'Maybe you are a little bit better,'" he recalled in an interview with Achievement.org. "'You may not have any extra talent, but maybe you are just paying more attention to what you are doing.' I think that's when I realized I was the sort of person that was objective enough and dedicated enough to do a good job. Then there was the challenge to keep doing better and better, to fly the best test flight that anybody had ever flown," he added. "That led to my being recognized as one of the more experienced test pilots and that led to the astronaut business."

In 1957, Shepard graduated from the Naval War College in Newport, Rhode Island. Upon graduation, he was given the position of aircraft readiness officer reporting to commander in chief of the Atlantic Fleet. As exciting as this was, it would pale in comparison to what was waiting just around the corner for him.

Although Shepard had already accomplished a great deal in his life, the best was yet to come. In 1959, he would be selected, through a long and involved process, for the biggest challenge of his life. Shepard would soon be leaving behind the navy and its fighter jets for the space capsules of NASA—the National Aeronautics and Space Administration.

CHAPTER 2

THE MERCURY 7 ASTRONAUTS

Whenever he was interviewed about his many accomplishments in life, Alan Shepard always first mentioned his selection as one of the original Mercury astronauts in April 1959. "That was competition at the best," he said. "Not because of the fame or the recognition that went with it, but because of the fact that America's best test pilots went through this selection process down to seven guys and of those seven, I was the first to go. That will always be the most satisfying thing for me."

It was a satisfaction that, at first, Shepard thought he might never get the chance to savor. In early 1959,

NASA screened the service records of more than 500 potential candidates for its new manned spaceflight program. In February, it sent a letter to 110 of the country's top test pilots inviting them to volunteer for the program. The *New York Times* ran a story about these invitations, and Shepard happened to see it. "I read the article on a Friday afternoon," he told Achievement.org, "and thought, I fulfill all these qualifications, I wonder where my invitation is? It was a rather miserable weekend of saying, 'Gosh, I wonder why they didn't choose me,'" he admitted. The following Monday morning, he found out that his telegram had been misplaced by the admiral's staff at the naval base where he was stationed. Though late in getting to him, Shepard had received an invitation from NASA.

Everyone who received an invitation and was interested in the possibility of spaceflight went to Washington, D.C., to be briefed. After NASA's presentation, each candidate had to decide if he really wanted to get involved in a manned space program. While some of them saw it as a once-in-a-lifetime opportunity, others saw it as an unexpected and not necessarily welcome career detour. At this time, the term "astronaut" was new and strange, and the space program seemed like science fiction to many people. A traditional career in the armed services seemed like a far safer and more sensible path to take.

Even Shepard's father discouraged the notion. His initial response to his son's interest was shocked disbelief. "Fortunately, in my case," Shepard told Achievement.org, "he lived long enough to see me go to the Moon and back. And one evening [after Shepard's return from the Moon], we'd had dinner, the ladies had retired, and we were having a drink in front of the fire, and he said, 'Remember when I said, "What are you going to do, son?"' I replied, 'Yes, sir.' And he said, 'Well, I was wrong.'"

Louise, Shepard's wife, took the news of her husband's potential new career move quite well. "She was all for it," said Shepard in the Achievement.org interview. "You know, being a test pilot isn't always the healthiest business in the world. I had been involved in testing off and on for six or seven years, flying stranger airplanes higher and faster than we could talk about and having done it reasonably successfully. They say any landing you can walk away

THE START OF THE SPACE RACE

Following the end of World War II, the United States and the Soviet Union, once allies, began entering into an ideological, political, and military struggle that affected nearly every other nation in the world. They had actually been disagreeing with each other since before World War I, mostly over their differing political and economic philosophies. The United States believed in democracy and capitalism, in which people are free to choose their own government and engage in the buying and selling of goods with little government intervention or oversight. The Soviet Union believed in Communism, which saw the government's role as imposing equality on all its people, partly by controlling the flow of money and goods so that extremes of wealth and poverty would no longer exist. Both nations wished to export their philosophies to other countries and create a world of like-minded nations. In order to counter each other's international efforts, both nations began building and amassing large stockpiles of weapons, including nuclear bombs and missiles. A tense military standoff developed between the two superpowers and their various allies.

All these issues came to a head on October 4, 1957, when the Soviet Union managed to launch its first satellite, *Sputnik I*, into space. This triumph was later followed by a brief Soviet manned spaceflight in 1961 by Yuri Gagarin in *Vostok I*. He became the first human ever to leave Earth's atmosphere and orbit the planet (a single orbit during a 108-minute flight). The United States was caught by surprise, having not realized that the Soviets possessed that technology. Americans were quite disturbed by these sudden developments, to say the least. For some, it was a full-fledged panic; it shook their faith in the competitiveness and capabilities of their own nation. The United States was not prepared to be beaten in this new space race, especially not by the Soviet Union.

Almost immediately, the American educational system began to put a greater emphasis on science and engineering in the classrooms. Technology became the nation's new focus as the United States found itself in stiff competition with the Soviet Union. The national space program accelerated in order to catch up with its rival. In a surprisingly short time, it did.

from is a good one. I think that she knew immediately that I would volunteer for it."

Making the Cut

The original group of 110 invited test pilots was slowly but methodically whittled down by NASA to a much smaller group of qualified candidates. Those who were taller than 5'11" (too tall to be able to fit into a capsule) or older than forty were out of the running automatically. Candidates had to have a bachelor's degree or an equivalent, be a qualified jet pilot, have at least 1,500 hours of flying time, and be in excellent physical condition.

Each of the remaining thirty-two interested candidates was put through a grueling series of physical, psychological, and emotional tests, ranging from probing personal interviews to full-body X rays. Each man was exposed to extremes of heat and cold as well as the powerful vibrations and noise typical of rocket blasts. They were isolated from each other, put through rigorous tests, and placed under extraordinary physical and mental pressure, all in order to find out whether they were strong enough

These are the Mercury 7 astronauts during desert survival training in Nevada. From left to right are Gordon Cooper, Scott Carpenter, John Glenn, Alan Shepard, Gus Grissom, Wally Schirra, and Deke Slayton. In addition to long johns, some of their makeshift clothing is made from parachute scraps.

to survive the extreme strain of space travel. The selection committee that ordered the tests and studied the results included everyone from test pilot engineers to flight surgeons and psychologists.

After all the tests were completed and the results were in, NASA was down to eighteen men who could be recommended with no medical restrictions.

Of those eighteen, the list was further narrowed down to the winning seven: Malcolm "Scott" Carpenter, Leroy Cooper, John Glenn, Virgil "Gus" Grissom, Walter "Wally" Schirra, Donald "Deke" Slayton, and Alan Shepard Jr. NASA announced the final roster of the so-called Mercury 7 astronauts to the press in early April 1959. For the next few months, the media watched the team's every move and eagerly awaited the announcement that would finally pinpoint who the main pilot would be on the United States's very first manned mission into space.

A National Obsession

The Mercury 7 team was introduced to the public at a press conference at the Dolly Madison House ballroom in Washington, D.C., on April 9, 1959. Immediately, the men that NASA had selected fascinated the press. They became the heroes of the day and were asked about everything, including things they knew little to nothing about. They were the darlings of the media, and everyone in America knew their names and the intimate details of their lives.

On April 9, 1959, NASA called a press conference in Washington, D.C., and introduced the Mercury 7 astronauts to the press and the American public. Seated from left to right are Deke Slayton, Alan Shepard, Wally Schirra, Gus Grissom, John Glenn, Gordon Cooper, and Scott Carpenter. All of these men would eventually reach space.

Although NASA tried to keep the country's obsession with the Mercury 7 team to a reasonable level, it did not work. Everywhere the astronauts went, cameras would flash and questions were asked. These brave new explorers definitely had the "right stuff," as author Tom Wolfe described it in his historical novel about the Mercury 7 team. The entire nation embraced these men and their courageous quest.

THE WORDS OF PRESIDENT KENNEDY

On May 25, 1961, President John F. Kennedy stood before Congress and challenged the entire nation to support a program that within a decade would put an American on the Moon and bring him back safely to Earth. It was considered one of his best speeches. This is an excerpt from his inspiring call to action:

I believe that this nation should commit itself to achieving the goal, before this decade is out, of landing a man on the Moon and returning him safely to Earth. No single space project in this period will be more impressive to mankind, or more important for the long-range exploration of space; and none will be so difficult or expensive to accomplish . . . In a very real sense, it will not be one man going to the Moon—we make this judgment affirmatively—it will be an entire nation. For all of us must work to put him there.

I am asking the Congress and the country to accept a firm commitment to a new course of action . . . If we are to go only halfway, or reduce our sights in the face of difficulty, in my judgment it would be better not to go at all . . . No one can predict with certainty what the ultimate meaning will be of the mastery of space. I believe we should go to the Moon. But I think every citizen of this country . . . should consider the matter carefully . . . and there is no sense in agreeing or desiring that the United States take an affirmative position in outer space unless we are prepared to do the work and bear the burdens to make it successful.

Kennedy was an enthusiastic supporter of space exploration. After Shepard returned from his momentous flight on *Freedom 7*, he met personally with Kennedy, and at the president's request, shared the exciting adventure with him. "We talked about the details of the flight, specifically how man had responded and reacted to being able to work in a space environment," said Shepard. "I tell you he was really, really a space cadet. And it's too bad he could not have lived to see its promise."

When three of the seven Mercury astronauts—Alan Shepard, John Glenn, and Gus Grissom—were chosen as the top candidates for pilot of the first American manned spaceflight, the Mercury 7 became known in the press as the Inner Three and the Outer Four. Not surprisingly, the Outer Four became largely ignored by the media as attention shifted to the Inner Three. When it eventually became apparent that Shepard was the one who would make that first historic flight, the focus intensified further on him.

Friendly Competition

The seven men on the Mercury team spent most of their days in training, classes, and lectures, learning all about emergency procedures and

Alan Shepard operates an early spaceflight simulator at Langley Research Center, in Hampton, Virginia, in 1960. Langley was the home base of Project Mercury, and Langley engineers became leaders of the project as well as of the later Gemini and Apollo programs. The Langley Research Center was responsible for training the Mercury 7 and designing and testing the Mercury capsule.

capsule hardware and operations. They also received a lot of valuable practice on a variety of flight simulators. In addition, each man focused on a specific technical task. Each task fell into one of three categories, corresponding to the mission's three main goals: to place a human spacecraft into orbital flight around Earth, to observe human performance under the unique conditions of space, and to recover returned astronauts and their spacecraft safely. Shepard chose to concentrate on the skills involved in recovery, the tasks and techniques necessary to pull astronauts and spacecraft out of the ocean after their reentry into Earth's atmosphere.

The competition between the seven on the Mercury team was fierce, but so was the camaraderie. As Wally Schirra once told John Christensen of CNN, "There was . . . always that sibling rivalry." The extremely difficult testing and education they all had to go through had strengthened the bond among the men, banding them together both as brothers and friendly rivals.

Tension built, however, as the team of seven waited for the selection committee to decide which one of them would be named lead pilot. Finally, on February 21, 1961, Robert Gilruth, director of Project Mercury, called a meeting of the team at NASA headquarters in the Langley Research Center in Hampton, Virginia. At the meeting, he announced that Shepard would be the mission's prime pilot, with Glenn as his backup pilot.

First Among Equals

It was a tough moment for each of the Mercury 7 astronauts. "Well, there I am looking at six faces looking at me and feeling, of course, totally elated that I had won the competition," recalled Shepard, in William Burrows's *The Infinite Journey*. "But yet almost immediately afterward feeling sorry for my buddies, because there they were. I mean, they were trying just as hard as I was, and it was a very poignant moment because they all came over, shook my hand, and pretty soon I was the only guy left in the room."

"I think it became obvious to all of us in that training period that Al was an extremely intelligent . . . dedicated leader whose motivation toward

accomplishing our mission was a true inspiration to all of us," stated John Glenn at a Washington news conference (as quoted by Tony Freemantle in the July 22, 1998, issue of the *Houston Chronicle*).

For the rest of their lives, the men of the Mercury 7 stayed in contact with each other on a regular basis. Gordon Cooper said to CNN's Christensen, "We're kind of like a bunch of brothers. We're quite close." Scott Carpenter added, "I always thought of us as 'All for one, one for all,' like the Three Musketeers. There's an abiding camaraderie that pleases everybody. It's the life of the group."

Even though the group now knew who was slated to head that first flight, the media had not yet been informed. Instead, they were told that three of the men were up for the job: Shepard, Glenn, and Grissom. In order to avoid an overwhelming

At top, the Mercury 7 stand before a Mercury capsule. From left to right are Gordon Cooper, Wally Schirra, Alan Shepard, Gus Grissom, John Glenn, Deke Slayton, and Scott Carpenter. At bottom, the seven astronauts pose in their Mercury space suits. In the front row *(left to right)* are Schirra, Slayton, Glenn, and Carpenter. In the back row are *(left to right)* Shepard, Grissom, and Cooper.

onslaught of media attention, Shepard's name was not announced as the winner until moments before he was scheduled to lift off.

John Logsdon, director of the Space Policy Institute at George Washington University in Washington, D.C., described Alan Shepard well when he told Robyn Suriam of *Florida Today*, "He was the embodiment of the 'right stuff'—a tough, straight-talking, risk taker. He had all the characteristics that we associate with the image of the astronaut hero." Logsdon was right, and the country would soon show its keen enthusiasm for Shepard—and for the entire space program.

CHAPTER 3

FREEDOM 7

By the time Alan Shepard and the *Freedom 7* capsule were finally ready to be launched, everyone at NASA was tense. The launch had already been postponed twice due to bad weather, so on the morning of May 5, 1961, many at NASA and around the nation were holding their breath in hopes that this time everything would go smoothly.

Launch Delays

Shepard woke up at one o'clock in the morning in preparation for the flight. He showered, shaved, and enjoyed a hearty breakfast of bacon-wrapped filet

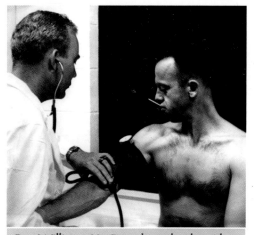

Dr. William K. Douglas checks Alan Shepard's blood pressure and temperature before the astronaut's historic *Mercury-Redstone 3* space flight on May 5, 1961.

mignon and scrambled eggs. Next, he had a final physical examination and was hooked up to biosensors that would monitor the effects of the mission on his body. He pulled on the 30-pound (13.6-kg) nylon silver space suit, picked up the portable air conditioner that ran cool air into his suit, and made his way to the rocket's launch pad.

Shepard officially entered the tiny capsule at 5:20 AM. The ten-story-tall, thirty-three-ton rocket was a modified Redstone ballistic missile. He climbed into the extremely cramped space and lay back on the formfitting couch. The countdown began at 9:34:13. Shepard was more than ready. He affirmed to mission control that everything was online.

"Roger, liftoff and the clock is started," he said to mission control, as quoted by Burrows. "Reading you loud and clear," replied Mercury 7 member Deke Slayton. "This is *Freedom 7*. The fuel is go. One point two g [force of gravity]. Cabin at 14 psi [pounds per square inch]. Oxygen is go."

Alan Shepard is escorted to the *Freedom 7* capsule before the launch of the *Mercury-Redstone 3* mission. Fellow Mercury astronaut Gus Grissom, at left, greets Shepard.

Although the countdown had finally started, it would be halted several times. The first time was when the sky clouded over. The countdown was stopped so that the photographers could get better pictures at liftoff. While they were waiting for the sun's return, another problem popped up. An electrical part had to be replaced, which took almost an hour. The countdown then resumed, but twenty minutes later it was stopped once again due to a computer error. Everyone on the ground was trying to fix the problem as fast as possible, but the wait was getting wearisome for Shepard since he had to stay in the tiny, cramped capsule. He finally snapped and said to the ground crew, "I'm cooler than you are. Why don't you fix your little problem and light this candle?"

By this time, Shepard had been sitting inside the capsule for hours, and he had a bit of a problem. He had to urinate. When he asked mission control what he should do about it, he received some simple, clear-cut advice: just let it go. According to John Moore of *Florida Today*, mission control reported, "No time to get Al to the bathroom, so he was advised to just let her go. And that he did, with fluid settling into and soaking the back of his space suit. Didn't bother him a bit." The urine managed to knock out a few of the biosensors and, of course, gave his colleagues material to tease him about for the rest of his life.

To the Stars

Finally, the countdown resumed, and this time around, it was not stopped. The launch went off without a hitch, with thousands of people watching in person at Cape Canaveral along with almost 50 million Americans tuning in to the live broadcast on television. What they saw was an enormous rocket being propelled up into the sky with the help of 75,000 pounds (34,019 kg) of thrust and 142 seconds of acceleration, all at six times the force of normal gravity. The *Freedom 7* capsule soon separated from its first-stage rocket and continued to climb, peaking at an altitude of 116 miles (187 km) and a speed of 5,134 mph (8,262 km/h). Although at this peak altitude Shepard experienced a full five minutes of weightlessness, he could not really feel the effects of it because he was so tightly strapped down. He described it all as "painless, just a pleasant ride."

One of the primary differences between Yuri Gagarin's 1961 flight in his *Vostok I* spacecraft and the *Freedom 7* was that the American rocket was not only manned, but it was steered and controlled using hydrogen peroxide jets. Gagarin was simply fired into space, orbited the planet once, and fell back to Earth without actually operating any controls or directing the operations of the craft.

Shepard's view, of course, was remarkable. "No one could be briefed well enough to be completely prepared for the astonishing view I got," he stated. "My exclamation back to Deke about the 'beautiful sight' was completely spontaneous. It was breathtaking." Shepard was often asked after his return from space what deep and philosophical thoughts he had while he was in *Freedom 7*. He usually pointed out that there was little opportunity to marvel at anything because he was kept so busy operating the capsule's controls and monitoring its flight. "Most of the time, something's happening," he explained in Chris Crocker's *Great American Astronauts*. "You're either launching or you're reentering or you're maneuvering in space. On that flight, I had about thirty seconds in which to look around and gaze upon the Earth from that altitude,

Mercury-Redstone 3, carrying Alan Shepard and the *Freedom 7* capsule, was launched on May 5, 1961. Shepard became the first American to complete a suborbital flight. The entire trip lasted only fifteen minutes.

see what it looked like, and make some kind of pro-
found statement."

The Man Who Fell to Earth

Shepard's brief, pleasant ride ended abruptly when
he and his capsule fell back into Earth's
atmosphere. "In that long plunge back to Earth," he
said, "I was pushed back into the couch with a
force about ten times the pull of gravity." The
pressure reached 11 g—eleven times the force of
gravity on Earth—and then the capsule's parachute
deployed. Shepard splashed down into the Atlantic
Ocean just over 300 miles (482 km) from shore.
The entire flight lasted fifteen minutes and twenty-
two seconds.

Shepard exited the floating capsule and was
hoisted aboard a marine helicopter and taken to the
aircraft carrier *Lake Champlain*. Physicians checked
Shepard thoroughly after his return. They found
him "disgustingly healthy." Before he had been
launched into space, they had been worried that his
body would not be able to withstand the rigors of
the launch and reentry. They were also concerned

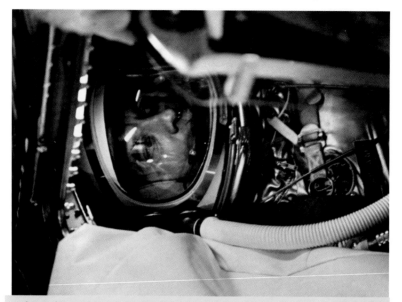

Alan Shepard sits inside the *Freedom 7* capsule. The *Mercury* capsule weighed about 2,000 pounds (907 kg) and was less than 7 feet (2.1 m) tall. Shepard reclined on a couch contoured to his individual shape. Heat shields protected both the capsule and Shepard from the 3,000°F experienced during reentry.

that the brief period of weightlessness would create mental or emotional stress. Fortunately, Shepard suffered from none of these problems.

After Shepard's return to Earth, he was treated as a national hero. Ticker-tape parades were held for him in Washington, Los Angeles, and New York. Each one drew hundreds of thousands of cheering people. President John F. Kennedy gave him the

Alan Shepard is met by a U.S. Marine helicopter and pulled up to safety following the splashdown of *Freedom 7* in the Atlantic Ocean, 300 miles (482 km) off the Florida coast. He and the capsule were flown to the nearby aircraft carrier *Lake Champlain*.

Distinguished Service Medal at a reception at the White House. When he went to hand the medal to Shepard, President Kennedy accidentally dropped it. Without missing a beat, the president leaned over and picked it up. With a smile, he told Shepard, "This decoration has gone from the ground up." Of course, so had Shepard.

An Astronaut Grounded

It would be quite some time before Shepard would see space again—something that neither he nor NASA expected. In 1962, the Mercury program was succeeded by Gemini. The Gemini space missions would focus on two-man, long-duration flights and docking technology as a run-up to the Moon landings of the Apollo missions. While training for one of the first Gemini flights, Shepard began to experience sporadic episodes of nausea, vomiting, and dizziness. The NASA physicians diagnosed him with an inner ear infection, and he was officially barred from any space missions until the condition was cured. He could not even fly an airplane unless a copilot was on board with him.

On May 6, 1961, one day after returning from space, Alan Shepard traveled to Washington, D.C. In a ceremony at the White House, he received NASA's Distinguished Service Medal from President John F. Kennedy. Shepard's wife, Louise, stands between the astronaut and President Kennedy.

This was a devastating emotional blow for Shepard, although he rarely ever spoke of it to anyone.

As time went by, Shepard's health problem did not improve or respond to traditional treatment. Finally, he returned to the physicians for further tests. This time he received a different diagnosis— Ménière's disease, an ailment that causes pressure to build in the inner ear. Very sensitive motion detectors are situated in this part of the ear, and they react negatively to the pressure. As a result, a Ménière's sufferer experiences ringing in the ears, vomiting, and severe dizziness. The problem is not considered very serious for most people, but it can end the career of a pilot or astronaut.

Since he was no longer able to fly, Shepard was appointed the chief of astronauts in the Johnson Space Center, in Houston, Texas. In this position, he was involved in every decision that concerned astronauts, from evaluating spacecrafts and monitoring pilots in flight-training programs, to deciding on future space expeditions and selecting the specific scientific experiments for each flight. He was greatly respected in this position, but his coworkers also knew that on any given day he could swing wildly from one mood to another. He was known equally for being the icy commander and the practical joker.

Jay Barbree, a veteran journalist who helped organize the material for the book *Moonshot*, told the *Houston Chronicle*'s Tony Freemantle, "His secretary had a picture of him hanging on the wall outside of his door. It was a double-sided picture—

one side was a smiling Alan Shepard and on the other side was a frowning Alan Shepard. When he came in in the morning," continued Barbree, "if he was in a bad mood, she'd flip over to the frowning side so that the astronauts knew it was probably best to come back another time."

Howard Benedict, a friend and cowriter of Shepard's later autobiography, summed it up this way, to Robyn Suriano of *Florida Today*: "He ran that astronaut office with an iron fist, but he earned the respect of astronauts, and I think that's one of his most memorable qualities—his leadership ability."

Although Shepard remained in this administrative position for almost a decade, he was frustrated. He wanted to leave Earth again. Fifteen minutes in space had not satisfied his strong desire to explore what lay beyond our planet. Finally, in 1968, when colleague Tom Stafford told him about a new type of surgery being done to correct Ménière's disease, Shepard thought he had finally found a possible solution to the problem that was preventing his return to space.

Later that year, he quietly left his home in Texas to check into a California hospital. Not wanting the media to know what he was doing,

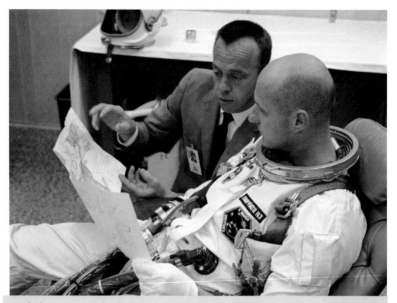

While grounded by Ménière's disease, Alan Shepard served as head astronaut coordinator at the Johnson Space Center in Houston, Texas. In this 1966 photograph, Shepard, wearing a jacket and tie, discusses the flight plan for *Gemini 11* with the mission's command pilot, Peter Conrad. *Gemini 11* blasted off on September 12, 1966.

he registered under the name Victor Poulis. He did not share his concerns or fears with anyone. "He kept those feelings very secret," Chris Kraft, former director of the Johnson Space Center, told Tony Freemantle. "He went off and had that operation performed, which was a very delicate one and a very unsuccessful one in many cases, by himself." Despite the risky odds, Shepard's surgery

"PROUD TO BE PART OF THE BEGINNING"

(Excerpted from *The Greatest Adventure: Apollo 13 and Other Space Adventures by Those Who Flew Them*)

"After considerable poking and probing, Scott Carpenter, Gordon Cooper, Gus Grissom, Wally Schirra, Al Shepard, Deke Slayton, and I survived the selection process . . . Much preparation followed, including many hours in a simulator that closely duplicated what we would see in the *Mercury* capsule. Al Shepard got the first mission, a sub-orbital flight, followed by a second sub-orbital mission by Gus Grissom. On February, 20, 1962, I made my flight aboard *Friendship 7*, a mission of three orbits—the first American orbital flight . . . I am indeed proud to have had the privilege to take part in the beginning of our outward reach into space."

—John Glenn

was a complete success, and months later he was considered fully cured. He regained much of the hearing he had lost earlier in his left ear. As a result, in 1969, Shepard was returned to full astronaut status. It was not long before Shepard was assigned to be the commander on the upcoming *Apollo 14* flight.

Training for this new mission took many hours of hard, exhausting work, as Shepard revealed to Chris Crocker. "The human mind can only comprehend so many details," he said, "and when you stuff more things into the memory bank, other things are bound to dribble out . . . You ought to try to cram it as full of the right things as you can right up to the last moment."

Before Shepard could return to space as the commander of the *Apollo 14* mission, however, three of his colleagues would attempt NASA's third lunar landing as part of the *Apollo 13* mission in April 1970. This was the fifth Apollo mission (the second since the first Moon landing), and nine years had passed since the first U.S. manned spaceflight sent Alan Shepard into space. In the interim, numerous Mercury, Gemini, and Apollo missions had been successfully completed. The country was beginning to take the space program for granted. NASA and its engineers and astronauts were doing their jobs so well that spaceflight was beginning to seem almost routine and error-free to the casual observer. The near disaster of *Apollo 13* would change all that and shatter the complacency of those on Earth.

CHAPTER 4

THE TERROR AND THE TRIUMPH OF APOLLO

On April 11, 1970, *Apollo 13* was launched with a crew of three: James Lovell, Fred Haise Jr., and John Swigert Jr. The mission's main objective was to explore the Fra Mauro highlands of the Moon's surface and collect lunar material and scientific data. The spacecraft was composed of three connected modules: command, service, and lunar. The command module (cm) contained the crew, spacecraft operations systems, and re-entry equipment. The service module (sm) carried most of the craft's supply of oxygen, water, helium, fuel cells and fuel, and its main propulsion system. The lunar module (lm) was the attached craft that was supposed to ferry the astronauts from their capsule to the Moon and back.

A little more than fifty-six hours into the flight—only minutes after the completion of a live broadcast on nationwide American television in which the astronauts led a tour of the command and lunar modules—an oxygen tank in the ship's service module ruptured unexpectedly. The explosion damaged several of the service module's propulsion, electrical, and life support systems. As a result, it no longer had enough oxygen, fuel, water, or electricity for the crew to return to Earth safely.

The entire world watched and waited while the Apollo crew in the air and on the ground raced to find a way to avert catastrophe and bring the astronauts home. The planned lunar landing was immediately aborted. *Apollo 13*'s only mission now was to find a way to return to Earth.

This is a photograph of the badly damaged service module of the *Apollo 13* spacecraft taken from the command module after the jettisoning of the service module. The inset shows *Apollo 13* commander James Lovell in the spacecraft's lunar module, into which the astronauts were forced to retreat to save oxygen and fuel.

Working the Problem

The crew was forced to use several ingenious strategies to conserve oxygen, fuel, and electricity. With oxygen supplies depleted in the command module, the astronauts took shelter in the lunar module, which remained unaffected by the explosion. In order to save precious electricity and fuel, they cut power to the lunar and command modules, preserving only basic essential functions, such as communications and airflow. The lunar module had small thrusters attached to it that were supposed to be fired when guiding it from the spacecraft to the Moon's surface and back. With fuel depleted in the service module, the astronauts were forced to use the lunar module's thrusters to send the spacecraft around the Moon and back into Earth's atmosphere.

In preparation for re-entry, the crew returned to the command module and powered it up (it had enough power remaining to carry them through the final two hours of their flight). They then jettisoned the service and lunar modules. Against all odds, the *Apollo 13* command module splashed down in the

Pacific Ocean on April 17, 1970, after a six-day mission filled with mishap, anxiety, ingenuity, and raw courage. It had been a very long week for all Americans.

Alan Shepard monitored communications between the *Apollo 13* astronauts and mission control during the spacecraft's crisis.

Commander Lovell looked upon the entire episode as a "successful failure." In *The Greatest Adventure: Apollo 13 and Other Space Adventures by Those Who Flew Them*, he wrote, "*Apollo 13* demonstrated the initiative and motivation of space engineers and technicians to salvage a crippled spacecraft under extremely demanding and trying circumstances. More personally, the excellent teamwork between the control center and the flight crew made it possible for me to tell the story."

The entire nation let out an enormous sigh of relief, and the can-do nature of the space program again captivated the country. In the wake of

THE RIGHT STUFF COMES TO THE SCREEN

Tom Wolfe's best-selling historical novel *The Right Stuff* was made into a movie in 1983. Although it did not do very well in the theaters, it was nominated for best picture of the year by the Academy of Motion Picture Arts and Sciences (which gives out the Oscars) and did quite well on video. The film was based on Wolfe's investigation into the early years of the manned space program and the multiple Mercury flights. The cast included Sam Shepard as Chuck Yeager, Scott Glenn as Alan Shepard, Ed Harris as John Glenn, Dennis Quaid as Gordon Cooper, and Fred Ward as Gus Grissom. The men are all portrayed as national heroes, and the film helped briefly to reignite interest in the space program. Enthusiasm for NASA's projects had flagged throughout the 1970s and early 1980s.

Apollo 13, new safety standards and other changes took place at NASA to prevent anything like that from ever happening again. *Apollo 14* would provide the first test of their effectiveness.

Shepard's Return to Space

Alan Shepard was to be the commander of *Apollo 14*, which, like *Apollo 13*, was a mission designed to explore the lunar surface of the Fra Mauro highlands and collect lunar material and scientific data. A new lunar vehicle, a two-wheeled cart, would allow the astronauts to cover more territory on the Moon and collect more samples.

Shepard's crew consisted of lunar module pilot Edgar Mitchell and command module pilot Stuart Roosa. While Mitchell and Shepard would be on the lunar surface performing experiments and collecting samples, it would be Roosa's job to conduct photographic and visual observations from the command module in orbit above the Moon. The *Apollo 14* mission was considered a real rookie mission; Mitchell and Roosa had no actual spaceflight time yet, and Shepard had logged only those brief fifteen minutes during the *Freedom 7* mission. In addition, due to the years Shepard was grounded by health problems, he was, at forty-seven, far older than the average astronaut. There was much speculation as to whether his age was an asset or a liability.

A High-Stakes Mission

Much was riding on *Apollo 14*, and NASA wanted to make sure this mission went well. After the near tragedy of *Apollo 13*, the nation needed reassurance that the space program was reliable and safe and that the value of its scientific discoveries made the risks of manned spaceflight worthwhile. NASA needed a successful mission to boost the national spirit, as well as restore the country's faith in the space agency.

This mission was also notable because of the vast number of experiments that were to be performed during the flight. Some of the goals included the first use of the mobile equipment transporter (a collapsible, two-wheeled cart that could carry tools, cameras, and lunar samples), placement of the largest payload ever in lunar orbit, the longest stay on the

Apollo 14 would take Alan Shepard to the Moon, land him on its surface, and allow him to explore outside the lunar module for hours on end. The *Apollo 14* crew is shown here, with Shepard flanked by Stuart Roosa, command module pilot, on the left, and Edgar Mitchell, lunar module pilot, on the right.

lunar surface by astronauts (thirty-three hours), the longest time spent outside of the lunar module exploring the Moon's surface (nine hours and seventeen minutes), and the first use of a color television camera on the lunar surface.

The *Apollo 14* mission was scheduled to launch on January 31, 1971. The countdown was delayed for forty minutes due to thunderstorms passing

In this November 4, 1970, photograph, Alan Shepard and Edgar Mitchell are seen in weightlessness training aboard an Air Force KC-135 plane. By climbing steeply and then entering a brief dive, this plane could create weightless-like conditions for thirty-second periods.

through the area. Once the weather cleared, the launch went perfectly—but not everything would go so smoothly.

While the *Apollo 14* crew certainly did not have to cope with any of the multiple life and death issues that *Apollo 13* did, it did run into a few serious problems. After being launched into orbit, the command module was supposed to separate from the final stage rocket that helped carry it into space. The lunar module was attached to this rocket, so once separation occurred, the command module would have to redock with the lunar module and pull it away from the spent rocket. Five attempts to dock with the lunar module failed because catches on the docking ring were malfunctioning. For a few moments, it seemed as if the lunar module would be lost and Shepard and Mitchell would not be able to land on the Moon. On their sixth attempt, however, they were able to forcibly drive the latches into place and successfully dock with the lunar module.

Landing on the Moon

The next important step in the mission was lunar separation—the release of the lunar module from the command module in advance of its landing on the Moon. The lunar separation went smoothly, but the lunar module's computer mysteriously went into abort mode, and the crew had to stop to reprogram it before moving forward. Later, during the eleven-and-a-half-minute drop to the lunar surface, the landing radar suddenly cut out, leaving the crew to

During Alan Shepard and Edgar Mitchell's first extravehicular activity on the Moon's surface on February 5, 1971, they stopped to photograph their lunar module. The flag they had raised upon landing is seen on the left. The lunar module landed in the Moon's Fra Mauro highlands, where *Apollo 13* was also supposed to have landed.

fly blind as they hovered above the Moon. They were about to cancel the landing when Mitchell simply flipped the radar switch on and off, and the system came back on. Everyone was relieved, especially Shepard. He had waited a long time for this very moment. His very first words as the lunar module landed on the Moon were simple yet profound, "I'm finally here."

The landing was perfect. When Shepard opened the hatch and stepped out onto the surface, he looked around him, gazed out at the Earth, and wept. He reported back to the ground crew, stating, "Al is on the surface, and it's been a long way, but we're here."

Getting Down to Work

Shepard and Mitchell were not merely walking around the Moon in awe and delight. They had an enormous amount of work to perform that would take them across 2.2 miles (3.5 km) of the lunar surface. At first, the men collected almost 100 pounds (45 kg) of dirt, rocks, and other samples to take back to Earth. It was painstaking and tiring work, especially since they were weighed down by heavy, bulky spacesuits. They had to work as a team to successfully complete all their tasks. Later, Mitchell said about Shepard, "We had a great mission together. He counted on me. I counted on him. We did what we set out to do and had a good time doing it . . . It was the common attitude: 'We get paid to do this?' As Shepard told the Associated Press, "It was the greatest adventure of a lifetime."

Alan Shepard stands next to the flag he has just planted in the Moon's surface in the shadow of the lunar module. This was the third American flag to be raised on the Moon, following the *Apollo 11* and *Apollo 12* missions. Edgar Mitchell's shadow can be seen at center bottom as he takes Shepard's picture.

Mitchell and Shepard conducted two seismic experiments on the Moon. One used a piece of equipment nicknamed the Thumper, a device that set off small explosions on the lunar surface. Its effects were measured by a machine called a geophone. The second experiment was to deploy a grenade launcher on the Moon to be activated by radio command after they returned safely to the command module.

The next project was a 1-mile (1.6-km) hike to the Cone crater. At first, things went well. The longer Mitchell and Shepard walked, however, the more disoriented and exhausted they became. They were pushing the mobile equipment transporter between them, which kept sinking into lunar potholes. The going was slow and tiring. To keep cool, they had to turn up the ventilation in their suits. Finally, they became too tired to go on. The two men turned around and returned to the lunar module, not realizing that they were less than 200 feet (61 m) from the crater that was their destination.

Before leaving the Moon to return to the command module, Shepard took a moment to complete another first for the NASA space program. He was passionate about the game of golf; the only thing more important to him was spaceflight. He regularly played in charity tournaments in the Houston area. Now that he was on the Moon, he could not resist taking a couple of swings. Using a golf club constructed from a

Edgar Mitchell is seen carrying a penetrometer near the unpacked Apollo Lunar Surface Experiments Package (ALSEP). The device was used to take soil measurements.

long-handled soil collection scoop with a golf head attached to it, Shepard hit two golf balls. It was the first game of lunar golf. The first ball landed in a nearby crater. The other, thanks to the gravity of the Moon, which is one-sixth that of Earth's, went on for miles and miles and miles, according to Shepard. He was rumored to have said, "Not bad for a 6 iron."

Returned Apollo astronauts were kept in quarantine so doctors could monitor their health. From left, Shepard, Mitchell, and Roosa are seen in their sealed quarantine trailer being greeted by their wives. From left are Louise Shepard, Joan Roosa, and Louise Mitchell. The *Apollo 14* crew was in quarantine for more than two weeks.

During the *Apollo 14* mission, Shepard logged nine hours and seventeen minutes outside the lunar module on the surface of the Moon, a record at that time. The mission ended on February 9 when the astronauts' capsule splashed down in the Pacific Ocean and was picked up by the aircraft carrier USS *Orleans*. The mission was considered a complete success—something the nation had desperately needed after the scare of *Apollo 13*. "*Apollo 12* and *14* proved that scientists could select a target area and define a series of objectives and that man could get there with precision and carry out the objectives with relative ease and a very high degree of success," said Shepard in Michael Collins's book *Liftoff*. The Apollo program was back on track, thanks in large part to the steady guiding hand and cool head of Alan Shepard.

CHAPTER 5

INTO THE
BUSINESS WORLD

Once again, Alan Shepard returned from space to a hero's welcome and a series of public celebrations. A ticker-tape parade was held in New York that drew more than 250,000 people, after which he was given the City of New York Gold Medal. Shepard was even awarded an honorary doctorate of science from Miami University in Oxford, Ohio, as well as an honorary doctorate of humanities from Franklin Pierce College in Rindge, New Hampshire. In addition to this, he was given the American Astronautical Society's Flight Achievement Award.

He accepted all these honors and tributes with great humility. Of his achievements in the space program, Shepard remarked in Crocker's book *Great American Astronauts*, "In the beginning there was a lot of glamour and excitement. It was new to the public. But there really wasn't that much to it." As great as his success was at NASA, it was equaled, if not surpassed, by the success he found after he left the space program behind and turned his sights to the business world.

In 1971, soon after Shepard's return from the *Apollo 14* mission, President Richard Nixon assigned the former astronaut to be a delegate to the 26th United Nations General Assembly. He served in that position from July until December of that year. In late 1971, he was promoted to rear admiral in the navy and soon after returned to his familiar job as chief of the astronaut's office at the Johnson Space Center. He remained there until he retired from both NASA and the navy on August 1, 1974. Shepard was just over fifty years old at the time of his resignation.

Life on Earth

Following his retirement from the government and the space program, Shepard immersed himself in the

business world. He became the partner and chairman of the Marathon Construction Corporation in Houston. After that, he became president of the Windward Distributing Company, a Houston-area Coors beer distributor. He joined the board of directors of several companies, became a partner in a venture capital group (these groups invest in new businesses), and was named director of a mutual fund company (a company that invests the money of its shareholders in a wide variety of corporations, stocks, and bonds).

In the following years, Shepard also established his own business, Seven Fourteen Enterprises, named after his two NASA spaceflights aboard *Freedom 7* and *Apollo 14*. This organization operated as an umbrella group for a number of other companies, all of which were relatively successful. Other interests included multiple investments in commercial real estate business ventures, quarter horses, banks, and oil wells. This involvement in such a variety of successful businesses, along with wise investments, helped Shepard to become a millionaire. He and his wife, Louise, owned homes in Houston; Breckenridge, Colorado; and Pebble Beach, California.

Six months after his return from the Moon, Alan Shepard was promoted by the navy to rear admiral. Navy Secretary John Chafee, at left, and Vice Chief of Naval Operations Admiral Ralph W. Cousins, at right, pin the stars to Shepard's shoulders on August 26, 1971.

Another project that Shepard became involved in was *Moon Shot*, a nonfiction book about the early years of the space program. Shepard's co-author was Deke Slayton, his friend and colleague from the Mercury days. Two veteran journalists helped the astronauts organize their information. The book covers everything from the close bond of the Mercury 7 team to

ESTABLISHING THE
MERCURY 7 FOUNDATION

In 1984, Shepard, along with other astronauts from the Mercury 7 team, helped to establish what they christened the Mercury 7 Foundation. Designed to raise money for science and engineering scholarships for students, the organization is located in Titusville, Florida. The new organization was headed by Shepard, who was elected founding president. It was a position that he would hold until 1997, when he would pass it on to astronaut James Lovell, commander of *Apollo 13*.

The name of the foundation was changed to the Astronaut Scholarship Foundation in 1995. The first scholarships were given out in 1986, and they continue to be awarded every year. Thanks to increased fund-raising and donations, the value of the scholarships has grown. While they once started at $1,000 each, they now commonly reach $10,000 each.

The foundation also serves as a consultant to the Astronaut Hall of Fame, which is located nearby at the Kennedy Space Center's visitor complex.

the space race with the Soviet Union and later Apollo missions.

Shepard's post-NASA life remained a full and busy one despite the fact that his days of walking on the Moon and traveling in a high-speed rocket were over. The last few years of his life followed the same pattern—this was a man who just kept pushing the envelope, even in retirement.

A QUIET ENDING

Despite his success in the business world, Alan Shepard maintained his ties to NASA and continued to support the space program and everything for which it stood. When there was serious discussion of cutting back the funds for the International Space Station (ISS; a large orbiting scientific research center, supported, built, and staffed by sixteen nations), Shepard protested, arguing that any attempt to kill funding for the station was shortsighted. He saw the ISS as a stepping-stone for endless future exploration. "The space station represents our future," he said. "Let's hope we still have what it takes to step up to that challenge. The dreams of our children are riding on it" (as quoted by Robyn Suriano).

Shepard was often called upon to comment on the progress of the space program, especially following the *Challenger* disaster of January 28, 1986, in which the space shuttle exploded minutes after liftoff. His position on the disaster and the proper response to it was philosophical. "Thirty years ago," he said, "the large percentage of the population thought we were crazy sitting on top of a rocket and allowing ourselves to be thrust into space. There was a lot of doubt . . . especially from some of the more learned members of the medical community who thought that man shouldn't be in space; it wasn't his place to be there. Had we said thirty years ago that we were going to put man in space for thirty years and we're only going to have two accidents, we would have said, 'Boy, we'll take that right now.' [The first fatal NASA accident occurred on January 27, 1967, when Gus Grissom, Edward White, and Roger Chaffee were killed in an explosion while testing their Apollo capsule]. Certainly, pushing out the frontiers as we did and still are doing, and having one accident in flight, the other on the ground, really is

More than a week after his death, on August 1, 1998, the four remaining Mercury 7 astronauts assembled for a memorial service for Alan Shepard at the Johnson Space Center in Houston. From left are Gordon Cooper, Wally Schirra, Scott Carpenter, and John Glenn.

remarkable" (as quoted by the *Los Angeles Times*). If Shepard had been present for the explosion of the space shuttle *Columbia* during reentry on February 2003, it is likely he would have still felt the same way and said the very same thing.

Beyond the Stars

While Shepard continued to argue on behalf of the space program, he was also battling something that could not be won over by his arguments or influenced by his celebrity: leukemia (an often fatal blood disease that leads to the overproduction of white blood cells). On July 21, 1998, he succumbed to the disease in a Monterey, California, hospital at the age of seventy-four. Friends and coworkers from all over the world mourned the loss of a national hero.

John Moore, fellow test pilot and personal friend, said in a *Florida Today* article, "Al was an exceptional man, a genuine friend, a natural hero, yet seemingly unaffected by fame. Same old Al. Thank you, old buddy, for all you gave us and our nation. You will not be forgotten."

NASA administrator Dan Goldin said, "NASA has lost one of its greatest pioneers, America has lost its shining star. Alan Shepard lived to explore the heavens. On this, his final journey, we wish him Godspeed" (as quoted by Robyn Suriano). President Bill Clinton echoed Goldin's sentiments when he said, "Those of us who are old enough to remember the first spaceflights will always remember what an impression he made on us and on the world. So I would like to express our gratitude of our nation and to say that our thoughts and prayers are with his family" (as quoted by the Associated Press).

Four weeks after her husband's death, on August 26, Louise, Shepard's wife of fifty-three years, died of an apparent heart attack while flying home to California after visiting her daughter in Colorado. Journalist Jay Barbree told R. Norman Moody of *Florida Today*, "Louise was the quintessential lady. She was just class. The perfect person." The couple's ashes were spread by a navy helicopter over Stillwater Cove in front of their Pebble Beach home in California. They were survived by three daughters, Julie, Laura, and Alice, and six grandchildren.

A Hero's Legacy

Shepard's passing inspired many bittersweet reflections on the history of the space program.

NO TURNING BACK

"We must somehow keep the dreams of space exploration alive, for in the long run they will prove to be of far more importance to the human race than the attainment of immediate material benefits. Like Darwin, we have set sail upon an ocean: the cosmic sea of the Universe. There can be no turning back. To do so could well prove to be a guarantee of extinction. When a nation, or a race, or a planet turns its back on the future, to concentrate on the present, it cannot see what lies ahead. It can neither plan nor prepare for the future, and thus discards the vital opportunity for determining its evolutionary heritage and perhaps its survival."

—James C. Fletcher, NASA administrator, 1975

John Logsdon, the director of the Space Policy Institute at George Washington University in Washington, D.C., said about Shepard, "[H]e and his Mercury colleagues were real heroes. They were path breakers. His death reminds us that we're in the transition away from the heroic age of spaceflight" (as quoted by Robyn Suriano).

During his lifetime, Shepard was the recipient of many awards, including the Congressional Medal of Honor for Space, two NASA Distinguished Service Medals, a NASA Exceptional Service Medal, the Navy Distinguished Flying Cross, and the American Astronautical Society Flight Achievement Award. After his death, the National Association of Educational Technology Specialists established the Alan Shepard Jr. Technology in Education Award. It is given once a year to a teacher (kindergarten through twelfth grade) who delivers excellent lessons in science and/or technology.

Alan Shepard Jr. has left behind numerous reminders of his achievement, courage, and adventurous spirit. His space suit from the Mercury mission hangs in the Smithsonian Museum in Washington, D.C. His handprints are cast in bronze at the Space Walk of Fame in Titusville, Florida. A future space shuttle was named after him in 2000—the USS *Alan Shepard*. A life-size statue of Shepard was dedicated in the rotunda at the Astronaut Hall of Fame at the Kennedy Space Center. Even though the man has been gone for years now, Shepard is still remembered with pride, affection, and honor by those who knew and worked with him. Gordon Cooper, a fellow Mercury flier, told Tony Freemantle, "He was certainly a very capable guy and a very capable astronaut. And of course, he was like a brother."

Shepard was the all-American representation of courage and determination. After all, he climbed into a rocket that had a reputation for exploding. He stuck to a lifelong dream of flight even when obstacles were put in his way. Yet despite his incredible number of life accomplishments, Shepard always remained humble. A CNN.com story entitled "Alan Shepard Was 'A Pretty Cool Customer,'" preserved Shepard's thoughts on his role in history. "During the actual process of flying spacecraft, or flying the *Spirit of St. Louis*, one doesn't think of one's self as being a hero or

On March 20, 2000, a life-size bronze statue of Alan Shepard was unveiled at the Astronaut Hall of Fame in Titusville, Florida, at the Kennedy Space Center. Assisting with the unveiling are two of Shepard's three daughters, from left, Julie Jenkins, Laura Churchley, and Alice Wackermann.

historical figure. One does it because the challenge is there, and one feels reasonably qualified to accomplish it. And it's later on, I suppose, perhaps, that you say, 'Well, yes, maybe. I must admit, maybe I am a piece of history after all.'"

At the memorial service for Shepard in Houston, George W. S. Abbey, director of the Johnson Space Center, summed up the man's life and legacy: "Alan Shepard is a true American hero, a pioneer, an original. He was part of a courageous corps of astronauts that allowed us to reach and venture into the unknown. Alan Shepard gave all of us the privilege to participate in the beginnings of America's great adventure of human space exploration."

GLOSSARY

agrarian Agricultural; relating to fields and farming.

ballistic missile A missile that has a highly arching trajectory, or flight path, and free-falls back to Earth after reaching the highest point of its ascent.

biosensor A device that is sensitive to physical and chemical stimuli—such as body temperature, heart rate, and blood flow—and transmits information about them.

camaraderie A warm spirit of friendship.

capsule A small pressurized compartment or vehicle.

claustrophobic Subject to the fear of small, narrow, or enclosed spaces.

deploy To place something in its proper position for effective use.

liability Something that represents a disadvantage or a drawback.

module Part of a spacecraft that is designed to
work with other attached components of the
craft.

orbit To revolve around or circle something.

payload The load carried by a vehicle, including
passengers, instruments, food, and water.

propulsion The action of driving something
forward with force.

roll A complete revolution of a plane or
spacecraft along its vertical axis as it continues to
fly forward horizontally.

seismic Relating to the vibration of a celestial
body, such as Earth or the Moon.

simulator A device that allows its user to
reproduce under test conditions the kinds of
situations and conditions likely to occur in a
real-life activity.

transatlantic Crossing the Atlantic Ocean.

FOR MORE INFORMATION

American Astronautical Society
6352 Rolling Mill Place
Suite 102
Springfield, VA 22152-2354
(703) 866-0020
Web site: http://www.astronautical.org

Goddard Space Flight Center
Code 130, Office of Public Affairs
Greenbelt, MD 20771
(301) 286-8955
Web site: http://www.gsfc.nasa.gov

Jet Propulsion Laboratory
Public Services Office
Mail Stop 186-113

4800 Oak Grove Drive
Pasadena, CA 91109
(818) 354-9314
Web site: http://www.jpl.nasa.gov

Johnson Space Center
Visitors Center
1601 NASA Road 1
Houston, TX 77058
(281) 244-2100
Web site: http://www.jsc.nasa.gov

Kennedy Space Center Visitor Complex
Mail Code: DNPS
Kennedy Space Center, FL 32899
(321) 449-4444
Web site: http://www.kennedyspacecenter.com

NASA Headquarters
Information Center
Washington, DC 20546-0001
(202) 358-0000
Web site: http://www.nasa.gov

Space Policy Institute
1957 E Street NW
Suite 403
Washington, DC 20052
(202) 994-7292
Web site: http://www.gwu.edu/~spi

U.S. Space Camp
P.O. Box 070015
Huntsville, AL 35807-7015
(800) 533-7281
(256) 721-7150
Web site: http://www.spacecamp.com

United States Strategic Command
Public Affairs Office
901 SAC Boulevard, Suite 1A1
Offut Air Force Base, NE 68113
(402) 294-4130
Web site: http://www.spacecom.mil

Web Sites

Due to the changing nature of Internet links, the Rosen Publishing Group, Inc., has developed an online list of Web sites related to the subject of this book. This site is updated regularly. Please use this link to access the list:

http://www.rosenlinks.com/lasb/ashe

FOR FURTHER READING

Cole, Michael D. *Astronauts: Training for Space.*
Springfield, NJ: Enslow Publishers, 1999.

Crocker, Chris. *Great American Astronauts.* New York:
Franklin Watts, 1988.

Deedrick, Tami. *Astronauts.* Mankato, MN:
Bridgestone Books, 1998.

Gibson, Edward, ed. *The Greatest Adventure: Apollo 13
and Other Space Adventures by Those Who
Flew Them.* Sydney, Australia: C. Pierson
Publishers, 1994.

Glatzer, Jenna. *The Exploration of the Moon: How
American Astronauts Traveled 240,000 Miles to the
Moon and Back, and the Fascinating Things They
Found There.* Vaughn, Ontario: Mason Crest
Publishers, 2002.

Gold, Susan D. *Countdown to the Moon.* New York:
Crestwood House, 1992.

Greene, Carol. *Astronauts Work in Space*. Minneapolis: Child's World, 1998.

Hayhurst, Chris. *Astronauts: Life Exploring Outer Space*. New York: The Rosen Publishing Group, Inc., 2001.

Johnstone, Michael. *The History News: In Space*. Cambridge, MA: Candlewick Press, 1999.

Kerrod, Robin. *The Children's Space Atlas: A Voyage of Discovery for Young Astronauts*. Brookfield, CT: Millbrook Press Trade, 1993.

Lassieur, Allison. *Astronauts*. Danbury, CT: Children's Press, 2000.

Sipiera, Diane M., and Paul P. Sipiera. *Project Mercury*. Danbury, CT: Children's Press, 1998.

Thompson, Kim M. *Space: Learning About Gravity, Space Travel, and Famous Astronauts*. Akron, OH: Twin Sisters Productions, 2001.

Wyborny, Sheila. *Astronauts*. San Diego: Lucent Books, 2001.

BIBLIOGRAPHY

Aaseng, Nathan. *The Space Race*. San Diego, CA: Lucent Books, 2002.

"Adm. Alan Shepard, Jr. First American in Space—Interview." The Academy of Achievement. January 16, 1997. Retrieved June 2003 (http://www.achievement.org/frames.html).

"Alan Shepard, First American in Space, Dies at 74." Los Angeles Times Online. July 1998. Retrieved June 2003 (http://www.teachspace.org/news/latimes/shepard.html).

"Alan Shepard Was 'A Pretty Cool Customer.'" CNN.com. July 22, 1998. Retrieved June 2003 (http://www.cnn.com/US/9807/22/obit.shepard.02/).

Burrows, William E. *The Infinite Journey: Eyewitness Accounts of NASA and the Age of Space*. New York: Discovery Books, 2000.

Chaikin, Andrew L. *A Man on the Moon: The*

Voyages of the Apollo Astronauts. New York: Viking Press, 1994.

Christensen, John. "The Mercury 7: Heroes, Rivals, Brothers." CNN.com. 2000. Retrieved June 2003 (http://www.cnn.com/SPECIALS/space/glenn/news/where.now).

Collins, Michael. *Liftoff: The Story of America's Adventure in Space.* New York: Grove Press, 1988.

Crocker, Chris. *Great American Astronauts.* New York: Franklin Watts, Inc., 1989.

Freemantle, Tony. "Friends Remember Moonwalker as Intelligent, Witty, Determined." *The Houston Chronicle.* July 22, 1998.

Godwin, Robert. *Apollo 14: The NASA Mission Reports.* Burlington, Ontario: Apogee Books, 2001.

Kranz, Gene. *Failure Is Not an Option: Mission Control from Mercury to Apollo 13 and Beyond.* New York: Simon & Schuster, 2000.

Launius, Roger D. *Frontiers of Space Exploration.* Westport, CT: Greenwood Publishing Group, Inc., 1998.

Launius, Roger D., and Howard E. McCurdy. *Imagining Space: Achievements, Predictions, Possibilities.* San Francisco: Chronicle Books, 2001.

Lovell, James, and Jeffrey Kluger. *Apollo 13.* New

York: Houghton Mifflin, 2000.

"Memorial Service for Alan Shepard August 1st." University Corporation for Atmospheric Research. July 30, 1998. Retrieved June 2003 (http://www.windows.ucar.edu/tour/link=/ headline_universe/ashepard.html).

Moody, R. Norman. "Alan Shepard's Wife, Louise, Dies." *Florida Today*. August 26, 1998.

Moore, John. "Fun and Friendship with Shepard 'Will Not Be Forgotten.'" *Florida Today*. July 28, 1998.

Quotes about Astronaut Alan Shepard. Associated Press. 1998. Retrieved March 2003. (http://www.chron.com/cgi-bin/auth/story.mpl/ content/chronicle/special/shepard/stories/quotes).

Reynolds, David West. *Apollo: The Epic Journey to the Moon*. New York: Harcourt, 2002.

Shepard, Alan, Deke Slayton, Jay Barbreee, and Howard Benedict. *Moon Shot: The Inside Story of America's Race to the Moon*. Paducah, KY: Turner Publishing, 1994.

Stott, Carole. *Space Exploration*. New York: Alfred A. Knopf, 1997.

Suriano, Robyn. "Alan Shepard, Astronaut, American Hero, Dead at Age 74." *Florida Today*. July 22, 1998.

INDEX

About the Author

Tamra Orr is a full-time writer living in Portland, Oregon. She is the home-schooling mother of four and has written more than a dozen nonfiction books for children and families.

Photo Credits

Cover, pp. 1, 33, 42, 46, 47, 50, 53, 54, 59, 65, 67, 71, 72, 74, 76–77, 79, 80 © NASA; pp. 4-5, 3, 11 © Hulton/Archive/Getty Images; pp. 8, 13, 21, 35, 85 © Bettmann/Corbis; pp. 16, 19, 20, 24 (inset), 56, 90 © AP/Wide World Photos; p. 24 © Corbis; p. 39 © Dean Conger/Corbis; p. 96 © AFP/Corbis.

Designer: Les Kanturek; Editor: John Kemmerer